Aviana's BAKING PROJECT

A Mother Daughter's Inspiring Journey into the World of Healthy Baking

AVIANA AND ARPITA CHINIWALLA

Balboa Press books may be ordered through booksellers or by contacting:

Balboa Press
A Division of Hay House
1663 Liberty Drive
Bloomington, IN 47403
www.balboapress.com
1 (877) 407-4847

Because of the dynamic nature of the Internet, any web addresses or links contained in this book may have changed since publication and may no longer be valid. The views expressed in this work are solely those of the author and do not necessarily reflect the views of the publisher, and the publisher hereby disclaims any responsibility for them.

Any people depicted in stock imagery provided by Getty Images are models, and such images are being used for illustrative purposes only.
Certain stock imagery © Getty Images.

ISBN: 978-1-9822-0151-7 (sc)
ISBN: 978-1-9822-0150-0 (e)

Library of Congress Control Number: 2018904100

Print information available on the last page.

Balboa Press rev. date: 10/16/2019

BALBOA.
PRESS
A DIVISION OF HAY HOUSE

Introduction by Arpita

This book documents a baking project completed by Aviana, my daughter, and myself. I set out to create a fun, educational experience through baking delicious, healthy treats. Each week we carefully shopped for the organic ingredients, baked, and photographed. Oh, I forgot to mention, we laughed in the process. And don't even get me started on the mess that was created!

Baking is my passion, and I wanted to share it with my daughter. At the time, I had just finished working with a health coach to figure out how to eat healthier. I learned gluten and refined sugar can be proinflammatory, which can wreak havoc all over the body. I quickly changed to a new way of eating that focused on organic, nutrient dense whole foods. Soon the whole family had adopted this way of eating.

Each recipe in this book is gluten free, refined-sugar free, and most are also dairy free. Not only did I enjoy baking with Aviana, but I had no problem allowing her to enjoy the treats because I knew they contained healthy, organic ingredients.

I recall the way Aviana lit up when we poured the batter or when she stole a chocolate chip and quickly put it in her mouth or when she took that first bite of a muffin she had worked hard to make. I have learned baking with a child is magical and healing. It is calming and changes a fussy moment into playful laughter. This cookbook is all about sharing the joy of baking with your child.

When I started the project, I didn't expect it would change me. I thought it would be a fun, educational activity to do with my daughter. However, week after week it changed me emotionally! As a mother, I found myself more present during and after our baking sessions in a way that transformed myself into a zen-like state.

So grab your son or daughter, turn up the heat in the oven, and get baking. And remember safety first! I always kept Aviana away from the stove and oven.

Be open, be amazed, and be there for your little ones.

Introduction by Aviana, age 6

Steps of baking by Aviana:
I love to bake.

Step 1—You need a small bowl and a big bowl and spoons.
Step 2—Put the dry ingredients in a small bowl and wet ingredients in a big bowl.
Step 3—Pour together and stir.
Step 4—You can pour in chocolate chips. I love them.
Step 5—Put those into trays with muffins, or you can make some cookies too.
Step 6—Take them out and eat them. *Yummy yum!*

Thank you. I'm happy for you to read this book.

—Aviana

Acknowledgments

Punit, my husband, who tirelessly watched the kids while I baked, wrote, photographed, and edited. You made this book possible.

My kids, my inspiration, my shining lights. Aviana you bring out my creative side! Baking with you is truly a joy. Niam, your smile lights up my world and keeps me young! As my main taste tester, you definitely contributed to this book. Both of you make my life so sweet.

Preety, without you, these healthy treats would have never made it into my world. Thank you for introducing me to healthy baking.

Lillian, you inspired me to take the plunge and put pen to paper. So grateful to you for believing in me even when I did not believe in myself. You have always been my guiding light.

Baking is my passion, and this book was so much fun to create.

My top ten tips for grain-free, gluten-free baking:

1. Gluten/grain-free treats are not as spongy as wheat/gluten containing treats.
2. Muffins do not bake in a classic dome shape.
3. In general, ingredients incorporate very well and quickly without much concern of overbaking.
4. To ensure muffins do not stick to the paper liners, spray the liners with coconut oil (or your oil of choice). Be sure to cover the liner completely with oil.
5. Do not expect the treats to taste like wheat/gluten containing baked goods.
6. Measuring flour is very important. Use the "dip and sweep" method or—even better—use a weighted scale.
7. I found sifting flour is easiest using a simple strainer.
8. Store flour in airtight containers in the refrigerator to prevent them from going rancid and to maintain optimal flavor.
9. Using unrefined sugars yields a subtle sweetness. I recommend training your taste buds to enjoy a mild sweetness or increase the amount of unrefined sugar to the desired level.
10. Calibrate your oven using an oven thermometer before you start baking. Each oven is different. Get to know yours!

This book is dedicated to moms, dads, and kids who want to experience the magic of healthy baking. Be ready to measure, mix, pour, bake, and *eat!* XOXO

General guidelines for purchasing ingredients:

1. Always buy ORGANIC and/or non-GMO when possible.
2. Use allergy friendly chocolate chips.
3. Superfine almond flour, coconut flour, and arrowroot flour can be purchased at most grocery stores including Whole foods, Trader Joe's or online through Amazon. Be sure to check expiration dates on all ingredients.

1. Avi's Molten lava cake—gluten/grain free

Aviana pushes me to be creative. She was looking through a cooking book when a picture of a molten lava cake caught her eye. She said, "Momma, let's make this." I tried to steer her toward one of my go-to muffins, but she insisted on the molten lava cake. So, I created my own healthier, gluten-free version. Enjoy!

Ingredients

For the cake:

¼ cup coconut flour
¼ cup coconut sugar
2 teaspoons baking powder
¼ teaspoon Himalayan pink salt
½ cup of allergy friendly chocolate chips
½ softened stick of unsalted grass-fed butter
⅓ cup whole milk
1 teaspoon vanilla extract
1 pasture-raised and/or organic egg yolk

For the lava:

1 tablespoon cacao powder
1 ½ cups of hot water

Garnish:

Whipped cream (page 15)
Berries
Nuts

Tools

Medium size glass mixing bowl
6 Silicone baking cups
Saucepan
Small mixing bowl
Baking sheet
Large mixing spoon
Measuring spoons

Baking tip

For thicker lava, add some almond, coconut, or whole millk to the cacao powder

Instructions

1. Preheat oven to 325 F.
2. In a medium bowl, mix together the coconut flour, baking powder, and salt.
3. Using the double broiler method, melt chocolate chips.
4. Once the chocolate chips are pretty well melted, add in butter.
5. Add melted chocolate chips and butter to the flour and mix well.
6. Add the milk, egg yolk, and vanilla to the chocolate batter.
7. Spoon the batter into each silicone cup. Fill about ¾ full.
8. Place silicone cups on the baking sheet. Bake for 20 minutes. Allow the cakes to cool for about 5–10 minutes.
9. In a separate bowl, mix together the cacao powder and hot water. Blend it well.
10. Flip one cake upside down onto a dessert plate and pour the hot cacao mixture over the cake to create the "lava."
11. Serve garnished with whipped cream (page 15), strawberries (or any berries), or nuts. The options are endless.

2. BAM BAM Blackberry almond muffins—gluten/grain free, dairy free

Who doesn't love a juicy blackberry? My kids just gobble them up. This recipe is my go-to during blackberry season. The combination of almond flavor pairs nicely with the blackberry. Always buy organic berries as pesticides really stick to berries.

Dry ingredients

¾ cup sifted superfine, blanched almond flour
⅓ cup sifted coconut flour
2 tablespoons sifted arrowroot starch
¾ teaspoon baking soda
½ teaspoon cinnamon
pinch of Himalayan pink salt

Wet ingredients

4 large pasture-raised and/or organic eggs
1 teaspoon vanilla extract
¼ teaspoon almond extract
3 tablespoons maple syrup
2 medium, brown-spotted bananas, mashed—about ½ cup
(The browner the banana, the sweeter the muffin will be.)
¼ cup coconut oil melted
½ cup coconut milk (if needed)

Add-in

1 cup fresh washed-and-dried blackberries

Toppings

½ cup raw sliced almonds

Tools

Medium size bowl—I prefer glass
Muffin pan
Muffin liners
Hand mixer
Spatula to fold in blackberries
Measuring spoons/cups
Toothpick

Baking tip

You can substitute coconut oil for any other oil you are comfortable baking with, such as sunflower seed or grape-seed oil.

Instructions

1. Position wire racks equally in the oven. Preheat oven to 350 degrees (or the equally calibrated temperature).
2. In a medium-sized bowl, combine the dry ingredients.
3. Add the eggs, vanilla extract, almond extract, maple syrup, and bananas and blend with a hand mixer until combined.
4. Slowly add the coconut oil to the bowl and blend well. If the batter is runny, let it sit for 5 minutes to thicken. Mix well. The batter should be smooth without any lumps—but not too runny.
5. Gently fold in the blackberries. Line muffin tins with paper cups. Gently spray each liner with coconut oil. Fill each muffin cup three-quarters full.
6. Sprinkle the tops of the muffins evenly with the sliced almonds.
7. Place muffin tray in the center of the middle rack. Bake the muffins for 15 minutes or until the toothpick comes out clean.
8. Place muffins on a cooling rack. Let them cool completely before eating.

3. Holiday Snickerdoodles—egg/grain/dairy free

These cookies scream holidays! I bake them up for holiday parties and then put them in a fancy holiday box with a bow. Aviana helps with the baking and decorating. She witnesses the importance of giving with love and care.

Ingredients

2 cups blanched, finely ground almond flour sifted and set aside
pinch of Himalayan pink salt
¼ teaspoon baking soda
5 tablespoons coconut oil melted
¼ cup raw honey
1 tablespoon vanilla extract

Cinnamon coating

½ tablespoon coconut sugar
1 tablespoon ground cinnamon

Tools

2 Medium-sized bowls—I prefer glass
Baking sheet or cookie sheet
Spatula
Measuring spoons/cups
Parchment paper

Baking tip

You can substitute coconut oil for any other oil you are comfortable baking with, such as sunflower seed oil, grapeseed oil, or grass-fed butter.

Instructions

1. Preheat the oven to 350 degrees F and line a baking sheet with parchment paper.
2. In a medium-sized bowl, combine dry ingredients and mix together well.
3. In a separate bowl, mix together the oil, honey, and vanilla.
4. Add the wet ingredients to the almond flour mixture and mix till combined. If time, refrigerate cookie dough for 20-30 minutes.
5. Combine the coconut sugar and the ground cinnamon in a small bowl.
6. Using a rounded tablespoon, scoop out the dough and then gently form into a ball. Roll in, or sprinkle all sides with, the cinnamon mixture.
7. Place the balls of cookie dough on a parchment-lined baking sheet, about 3 inches apart.
8. Using your hands starting at the center of the cookie, slightly flatten each cookie. Aviana really enjoyed this part. It was one big sticky mess!
9. Bake for 9-12 minutes. Place cookies on a cooling rack before enjoying them.

4. Monkey muffins: Chocolate chip banana muffins with walnuts—gluten/grain free

Makes 12 muffins

These muffins require BROWN bananas. The browner the banana, the sweeter the muffin. This recipe will allow you to use up those last few bananas from the week. If your bananas are not ripe enough, place them in the oven at 250 degrees F for 10–15 minutes. The peel will turn black. This is okay. Inside, the banana starch will have quickly converted to sugar, which is prefect for muffin making. Aviana enjoyed learning the difference between brown, yellow, and green bananas.

Dry ingredients

½ cup coconut flour sifted and set aside
½ cup tapioca flour sifted and set aside
1 teaspoon baking soda

Wet ingredients

½ cup melted grass-fed butter
½ cup coconut sugar—can omit if you prefer a lightly sweet muffin
1 cup very ripe bananas, mashed
1 teaspoon vanilla extract
4 large pasture-raised and/or organic eggs

Add-ins

½ cup allergy friendly chocolate chips
½ cup chopped walnuts

Tools

Medium size bowl—I prefer glass
Muffin pan
Muffin liners
Hand mixer
Spatula—to fold in chocolate chips
Measuring spoons/cups
Toothpick

Baking tips

Make sure eggs and butter are brought to room temperature. You can substitute butter for any other oil you are comfortable baking with, such as coconut, sunflower seed or grape-seed oil.

Instructions

1. Preheat oven to 350 degrees. Line a standard muffin tin with paper liners. Spray liner with coconut oil.
2. In a large bowl, whisk together coconut flour, tapioca flour, and baking soda.
3. In another large bowl, whisk together butter, sugar, bananas, vanilla extract, and eggs.
4. Combine the dry ingredients slowly into the wet ingredients while whisking the wet ingredients.
5. Gently fold in the chocolate chips and walnuts. Divide batter among the lined muffin cups, filling each muffin liner about 3 quarters full.
6. Bake until the muffins have slightly puffed, and the edges have slightly browned, about 20 minutes or until toothpick comes out clean.
7. Allow muffins to cool completely on a cooling rack.

5. Chocolate ZUC-chini muffins—gluten/grain free and dairy free

Aviana's initial reaction to the muffins were, "What zucchini! Mom!" I told her to just try one bite, and if she didn't like it, she didn't have to eat them. Of course, after the first bite, she smiled and said, "Yummy."

Dry ingredients

¼ cup sifted coconut flour
¼ teaspoon Himalayan pink salt
¼ teaspoon baking soda
1 teaspoon cinnamon

Wet ingredients

2 large pasture-raised and/or organic eggs
¼ cup melted coconut oil
¼ cup raw honey
1½ cups grated zucchini (don't pack down)

Add-ins

1½ cup allergy friendly chocolate chips or raisins

Tools

Medium-sized bowl—I prefer glass
Muffin pan
Muffin liners
Hand mixer
Spatula—to fold in chocolate chips
Measuring spoons/cups
Toothpick
Paper towels

Baking Tips

The key is to dry the zucchini thoroughly. Do not allow for excess water. Plan ahead, and grate zucchini one day ahead of time.

Take the time to bring eggs and flour to room temperature before mixing and baking.

You can substitute coconut oil for any other oil you are comfortable baking with, such as sunflower seed oil, grape-seed oil, or grass-fed butter.

Instructions

1. Preheat oven to 350 degrees.
2. Shred zucchini and measure, don't pack down, and then absorb extra liquid with paper towels. This step is very important. Do not skip.
3. In a medium bowl, combine eggs, oil, honey, and zucchini. Mix dry ingredients into wet ingredients thoroughly. The batter should not have any lumps. Stir in chocolate chips or raisins.
4. Line a mini-muffin pan or regular muffin pan with a muffin liners. Lightly spray or spread the coconut oil on each liner.
5. Spoon batter into muffin tin, filling just over halfway. Cook for about 18–22 minutes or until toothpick inserted comes out clean. These muffins rise very little. Be sure to cool muffins before eating.

6. Monkey Banana Bread—gluten/grain free and dairy free

Is there any bread more loved than banana bread? It makes for a delish breakfast, snack, or afternoon treat. Aviana would enjoy eating it right out of the oven. Please beware this banana bread will make your whole house smell divine.

Wet ingredients

4 medium-sized ripe bananas
4 large pasture-raised and/or organic eggs
4 tablespoons of coconut oil, melted
1 teaspoon vanilla extract

Dry ingredients

½ cup + 3 tablespoons of sifted coconut flour
¼ cup + 3 tablespoons of sifted superfine almond flour
1 teaspoon baking powder
1 teaspoon baking soda
1 tablespoon (heaping) of ground cinnamon
Pinch of freshly ground nutmeg
Pinch of Himalayan pink salt

Add-ins

Allergy friendly chocolate chips
Raisins
Walnuts

Tools

Bread pan
Vitamix or hand mixer
1–2 medium-sized glass bowls
Wooden spoon or spatula

Baking tips

Bring eggs, bananas, and flours to room temperature before mixing, otherwise coconut oil may chunk up.

The size of the banana matters. If using a large banana, adjust the baking time.

You may use grass-fed butter, sunflower seed oil, or grapeseed oil in place of coconut oil

Instructions

1. Preheat the oven to 350 degrees.
2. Grease a bread loaf pan with coconut oil/butter.
3. Combine all the wet ingredients into the Vitamix—or glass bowl if using hand mixer.
4. Combine and sift all dry ingredients into a large mixing bowl.
5. Pour the mixed wet ingredients into the large bowl of dry ingredients.
6. Mix well with a wooden spoon or spatula until the batter has come together.
7. Mix in your add-ins gently.
8. Pour the dough into your lightly greased pan.
9. Bake at 350 for 40–50 minutes. Place bread pan in the center of oven on the middle or top rack. Rotate pan ½ way through bake time. Be sure to check on bread after 30 minutes as individual bake times can vary.
10. Let the bread cool completely before slicing. Enjoy plain or with your favorite nut butter or fruit preserves.

7. A Touch of Green nut-free protein muffin—gluten/grain free and dairy free

Makes 12 regular-sized muffins. Each muffin contains 6 grams of protein.

Don't let the name fool you. These muffins are moist, lightly sweet, and completely satisfying. Aviana and I made these for her preschool class picnic, and they were a huge hit! One thing about this muffin is that it can turn green—perfect for St. Patrick's Day. Aviana was so surprised to see the green color and asked me why did they turn green? I investigated this. I learned the chlorogenic acid (chlorophyll) in sunflower seeds reacts with the baking soda or baking powder when baked and causes a green color when the muffin cools. Aviana was fascinated by this little science experiment. Don't let the green color stop you from trying the muffin. I have some tips below on how to minimize the green color.

Wet ingredients

1 cup sunflower seed butter
2 medium-sized, overly ripe bananas or approximately ⅔ cup of smashed bananas
2 large pasture-raised and/or organic eggs
1 teaspoon vanilla
2 tablespoons of raw honey
½ teaspoon baking soda
1 teaspoon apple cider vinegar
2 teaspoons cinnamon

Add-ins

Cacao chips, allergy friendly chocolate chips, dried cranberry, raisins, blueberries, raspberries, the options are endless

Tools

Vitamix or hand mixer
Muffin pan
Wooden spoon or spatula

Baking tips

Can substitute any nut butter in place of sunflower seed butter. When using sunflower seed butter, you may have to reduce baking soda and baking powder by about one-third to avoid green color.

Instructions

1. Preheat oven to 375 degrees F.
2. Place all ingredients into a Vitamix—or glass bowl if to be mixed with hand mixer.
3. Blend until well mixed.
4. Place cupcake liners into muffin tin. Spray each liner with coconut oil.
5. Pour batter into a cupcake liners.
6. Carefully sprinkle add-ins to each muffin and gently stir.
7. Bake for 15 minutes or until toothpick comes out clean.
8. Allow muffin to cool completely on a cooling rack before eating.

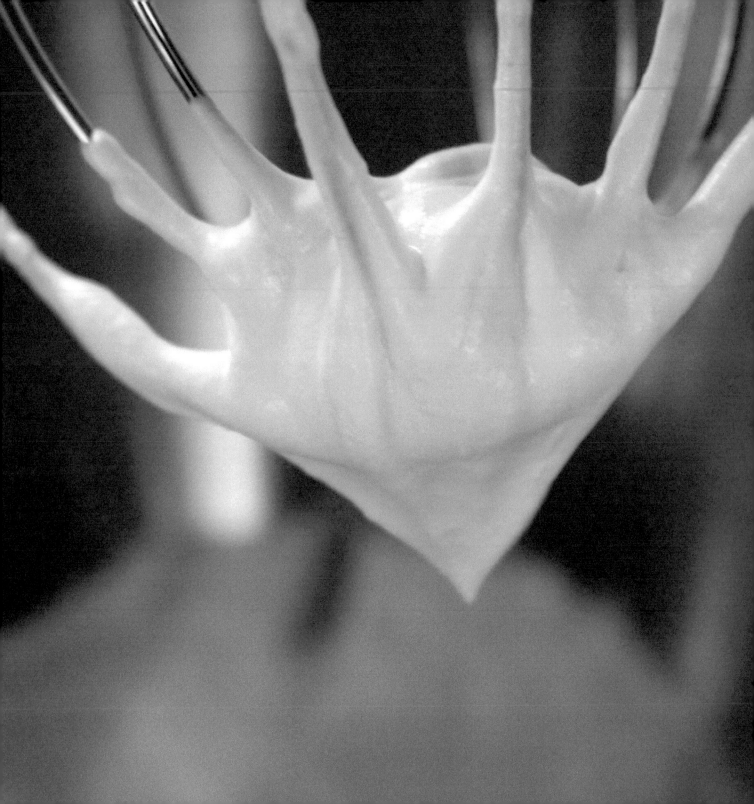

8. Whipped cream—dairy free

Ingredients

1½ cups chilled coconut cream. Trader Joe's has a good one
2 tablespoons Grade B maple syrup or coconut palm sugar
1½ teaspoons vanilla extract

Tools

Stand mixer

Baking tips

If you are unable to find coconut cream, you can make it: refrigerate 2 cans of coconut milk overnight for one or two nights. Open cans and scoop off firm top layer being sure to only get the cream.

Pairs well with fruit or cake. Can use in place of frosting on cupcakes or in hot chocolate.

Instructions

1. Place the cream in the bowl of a stand mixer or a large bowl.
2. Turn your stand mixer or hand mixer to high speed and whip the coconut cream for 3 to 5 minutes or until it becomes fluffy and light with soft peaks. Mix in maple syrup/coconut sugar and vanilla. Stores well in airtight container in the refrigerator for 2–3 days.

9. Healthy Holiday Chocolate Bark

This chocolate treat is perfect for Christmas or Valentine's Day. You can give them out as gifts too. Aviana and I made some for her teachers. It is super simple to package either in a Mason jar or candy box. Then complete the look by adding a ribbon. This recipe has the option to add-in goji berries which are considered to be a superfood. Goji berries are packed with nutrients including Vitamin A and C. Also, they are a great alternative to other dried fruit due to their low sugar content.

Makes one 9 x 12 sheet

Ingredients

1 pound allergy friendly dark chocolate chips
2 teaspoons coconut oil + extra for greasing

Add-ins

½ cup dried goji berries or unsweetened cranberries
½ cup shelled pistachios
¼ cup large toasted flakes of unsweetened coconut

Tools

9 x 12 baking sheet
Parchment paper
Saucepan

Baking tip

Store the chocolate bark in freezer to preserve freshness.

Instructions

1. Coat a 9 x 12 rimmed baking sheet with coconut oil cooking spray (or manually with paper towel and coconut oil) and then line with parchment paper, leaving an overhang on the long sides.
2. In a saucepan, melt chocolate with 2 teaspoons coconut oil over low heat until it is completely melted, mixing frequently to avoid sticking to the pan. Do not take your eyes off the saucepan, remove from heat as soon as the chips look like they have started to melt. Pour melted chocolate into the parchment-lined baking sheet.
3. Sprinkle add-ins over chocolate and very gently press toppings into chocolate so they don't fall off. Refrigerate or place in freezer until firm, at least 1 hour. Remove and break or slice into small pieces, and the bark is ready to serve.

10. Yummy in the Tummy chocolate chip cookies—gluten/grain free

12 medium size cookies

These cookies will fly off your table in a quick minute. Aviana loves making them. Often times they are gone in a day or so, and she is hunting for more. Enjoy!

Ingredients

¼ cup grass-fed butter brought to room temperature
¼ cup coconut palm sugar
2 tablespoons honey
1 large pasture-raised and/or organic egg, room temperature (be sure to bring to room temperature) + one egg white
2 teaspoons vanilla
1½ cups superfine blanched almond flour
½ teaspoon baking soda
½ teaspoon Himalayan pink salt
¼ cup allergy friendly dark chocolate chunks
¼ cup allergy friendly chocolate chips

Tools

Stand mixer
Spatula
SilPat or cookie sheet and parchment paper

Baking tips

Bring ingredients to room temperature for best results. Use superfine ground almond flour.

Instructions

1. Preheat oven to 350 degrees F. If using a cookie sheet, line with parchment paper.
2. In a food processor, cream the butter, coconut sugar, honey, vanilla for about 15 seconds until smooth and fluffy. Then add in eggs until well combined.
3. Add the almond flour, baking soda, and pink salt and mix again for about 30 seconds. Scrape down the sides of the bowl if needed in order to incorporate all of the flour.
4. Stir in the chocolate chips by hand.
5. Place about a tablespoon size of dough on a cookie sheet lined with parchment or a SilPat about two inches apart. Flatten balls until desired size.
6. Bake for 12–15 minutes, until slightly golden around the edges. Cookies will be very soft out of the oven and will slightly harden as they cool. Bake times may vary.
7. Places cookies on a cooling rack before eating.

11. Triple B's black bean brownies—gluten and dairy free

No one will know the secret ingredient in these brownies, which are loaded with protein and fiber. The only problem making them with your kids is they may refuse to eat after seeing the black beans. Try at your own risk!

Ingredients

1 (15.5 ounce) can black beans, rinsed and drained
3 large pasture-raised and/or organic eggs
3 tablespoons coconut oil
½ cup cocoa powder
⅓ gluten free quick oats
¼ teaspoon Himalayan pink salt
3 teaspoons vanilla extract
1 teaspoon baking powder
½–¾ cup sweetener of your choice (honey, sugar, agave, etc.)

Add-in

Allergy friendly chocolate chips—can either place into the batter or sprinkle on top

Tools

Vitamix or food processor
Spatula
8 x 8 square baking pan

Baking tips

After baking, if brownies seem uncooked, place in fridge and they will firm up. In terms of texture the brownies will be more fudge-like then cake-like.

Instructions

1. Preheat oven to 350 degrees F. Spray an 8 x 8 square baking dish with coconut spray or other oil.
2. Combine the black beans, eggs, oil, cocoa powder, quick oats, salt, vanilla extract, and sweetener in a blender. Be sure to blend well until batter is smooth.
3. Pour the mixture into the prepared baking dish. Add in chocolate chips.
4. Bake in the preheated oven until the top is dry and the edges start to pull away from the sides of the pan, about 25–30 minutes.

12. Happy Birthday vanilla cake —gluten/ grain free and dairy free

Wet ingredients

1 can white beans, rinsed and dried
6 large pasture-raised and/or organic eggs, slightly beaten—be sure to bring to room temperature
1½ teaspoons pure vanilla extract
⅓ plus 3 tablespoons cup raw honey (add more to make sweeter)

Dry ingredients

¼ cup coconut oil, melted
⅓ cup coconut flour, sifted
1 teaspoon baking soda
1 teaspoon baking powder

Tools

Vitamix
Springform pan
Muffin pan for cupcakes
Cupcake liners

Add-ins

Can use fruits, dried fruit, or chocolate chips— options are endless.

Baking tips

The beans may have salt; however, if they don't add ¼ teaspoon Himalayan pink salt along with dry ingredients.

Instructions

1. Put wet ingredients into the Vitamix and purée well.
2. Add dry ingredients into wet ingredients and purée well.
3. Pour into springform pan lined with unbleached parchment paper on the bottom and greased all around. For cupcakes spray each liner with coconut oil.
4. Bake at 325 degrees for about 30 – 35 minutes for cake. Check if done by inserting a toothpick into the center. If it comes out mostly clean, it's done. Bake for about 22-25 minutes for cupcakes—use toothpick test. Oven times may vary.
5. If desired, frost after cake or cupcakes have completely cooled.

Printed in the United States
By Bookmasters